Elementary Languages

Elementary Italian Grammar
for Reading & Writing
(with exercises)

Italiano elementare

Other books from Elementary Languages

Available in print and Kindle formats:

Elementary Readers (*Italian, Spanish, French*)

Elementary Spanish Grammar For Reading & Writing
(*with Exercises*)

Elementary French Grammar For Reading & Writing
(*with Exercises*)

Available in print only:

Vocabulary Review in Word-Search Puzzle Form
(*Italian, Spanish, French*)

www.elementarylanguages.com

Elementary Italian

Elementary Italian Grammar for Reading & Writing (*with exercises*)

by Philippe Delannoy, Ph.D. and Gabriella Marconi-Merriman, M.A.

Copyright © 2010 by Elementary Languages

ISBN 978-1-4528169-0-6

TABLE OF CONTENTS

Elementary Italian Grammar for Reading and Writing

Introduzione - *Introduction*

Welcome to the <u>Elementary Italian Grammar for Reading and Writing (*with exercises*)</u> ! This grammar book will get you started on the discovery of the Italian language with a step-by-step approach to language learning, with each lesson building on the preceding one. All lessons are connected in a logical sequence designed to make your learning experience at once satisfying and rewarding. Every concept, amply illustrated with meaningful examples, will show you the grammatical underpinnings of the Italian language, one step at a time. The vocabulary in each lesson reflects that lesson's theme (*e.g. greetings, numbers, verbs, etc*), thus allowing you to concentrate on specific aspects of the language. As you progress through this grammar book, you will build up not only a useful vocabulary, but you will know how and when to use it, wether it be simply for reading, writing, or eventually speaking the language.

Since this is an Elementary Grammar, the first lesson starts at the most basic level, with a short vocabulary list and a few grammatical points. At first, each example is given in both Italian and English, although the vocabulary given at the beginning of each lesson, coupled with the grammatical explanations, is sufficient to figure out the meaning of the examples. Starting with **Lezione 3**, some examples will be in Italian only. But by that time, you will find little difficulty, if any, reading and understanding the examples.

It is important to be patient when learning a new language. Take the time to read *slowly* and *carefully* each explanation and its accompanying examples. Never hesitate to go back to a previous lesson to check your understanding of a point of grammar.

Do not confine yourself to the examples given in a lesson. Write your own! Naturally, since each lesson ends with a few exercises, you will be able to practice reading and writing Italian right from the start.

You will see that each lesson uses something of the previous lessons to build new expressions and sentences. With that in mind, pay special attention to the sections titled **Putting Things Together.** It will not take long before you can read and write what at first may have appeared too difficult to tackle.

Do not be intimidated by long sentences! Each one can easily be broken down into its constituent parts. Look up any word that is not clear in the vocabulary list given at the beginning of each lesson. Write out the vocabulary from each lesson on a separate sheet of paper, adding on to your list as you go through the book. This is the first and the easiest writing exercise when learning a new language. It is usually easier to remember what you have written down than something you have only read.

When learning a new language, practice does indeed make perfect. For example, after doing the exercises for a lesson, go ahead and redo any exercise you have completed in previous lessons. Write your own sentences as often as possible. The more you use what you have learned, the better you will remember it and be able to use it spontaneously.

Buona fortuna ! - Good luck!

Lezione 1 - Benvenuti a tutti ! - (*Welcome to everyone !*)

Vocabulary

bambina	=	girl
bambino	=	boy
cane	=	dog
gatto	=	cat
e	=	and
il	=	the (*m.*)
la	=	the (*f.*)

Gender

Words in Italian are either **masculine** or **feminine**.
Masculine and Feminine are the only two **genders**
in Italian.

Example:	**Il** bambino	=	**The** boy (*m.*)
	La bambina	=	**The** girl (*f.*)

- **Il** and **La** are definite articles. They both mean **The**.

- **Il** is placed before a masculine word, and **La** before a
  feminine word.

- **Il** is the masculine definite article, and **La** is the
  feminine definite article.

The Conjunction E

The Italian word **E** stands for the English word **AND**

Example:

La bambina **e** il bambino	=	The girl **and** the boy
Il gatto **e** il cane	=	The cat **and** the dog

Things to do - Lezione 1

Use a separate sheet of paper to write
the following expressions in Italian.

1. The dog.

2. The girl.

3. The cat.

4. The boy.

5. The cat and the dog.

6. The girl and the boy.

7. The dog and the cat.

8. The boy and the girl.

Answers on page 41

Lezione 2 - Dentro la casa... — (*In the House...*)

Vocabulary

La casa	=	The house
C'è...	=	There is...
dentro	=	in; within; inside
un	=	a; one (*m.*)
una	=	a; one (*f.*)

The Indefinite Article

◆ The indefinite article **UN** stands for **A**

Un gatto = **A** cat

◆ **UNA** is the feminine form of **UN**

Una bambina = **A** girl

◆ **UN** and **UNA** also stand for **ONE**

Un bambino	=	**One** boy; **A** boy
Una bambina	=	**One** girl; **A** girl

C'è...

◆ The expression **C'è...** stands for **There is...**

Example... **C'è** un gatto dentro la casa.
There is a cat in the house.

Putting things together

You are now ready to read and write complete sentences in Italian:

Example: C'è un bambino e un cane **dentro** la casa.

- There is a boy and a dog **in** the house.

Things to do - Lezione 2

Use a separate sheet of paper to write
the following expressions in Italian.

1. There is a cat in the house.

2. There is a girl and a dog in the house.

3. There is a boy in the house.

4. There is one cat and one dog in the house.

Answers on page 41

Lezione 3 - I numeri da 1 a 10

(*The Numbers from 1 to 10*)

Vocabulary

uno	=	one	Una chiave	=	A key
due	=	two	Una finestra	=	A window
tre	=	three	Una sedia	=	A chair
quattro	=	four	Una tavola	=	A table
cinque	=	five	Ci sono...	=	There are...
sei	=	six			
sette	=	seven			
otto	=	eight			
nove	=	nine			
dieci	=	ten			

NUMBERS

♦ As you have seen in Lezione 2, **UN** and **UNA** stand for both **A** and **ONE**.

♦ The number **UNO** [1] in Italian is the **only** number with both a masculine and a feminine form: **UN** and **UNA**.

[1] *Use* **UNO** *only when saying the number by itself.*

Example:

Un bambino e **una** bambina = **One** boy and **one** girl

But...

Due bambini e **due** bambine [2] = **Two** boys and **two** girls

[2] *Notice the different endings for the plural words.*
See page 12 for details about the plural in Italian.

Plural Words in Italian

The plural in Italian is not the same as the plural in English. Instead of adding a **S** at the end of a plural word, the final letter changes according to the last letter of the singular form of that word, as shown in the examples below.

◆ When a singular word ends with the letter **o**, the plural form of that word ends with the letter **i**:

    Un bambin**o**   -   A boy; One boy
    Due bambin**i** -   Two boy**s**.

- -

◆ When a singular word ends with the letter **a**, the plural form of that word ends with the letter **e**:

    Una cas**a**   -   A house; One house
    Due cas**e**   -   Two house**s**.

- -

◆ When a singular word ends with the letter **e**, the plural form of that word ends with the letter **i**:

    Una chiav**e**   -   A key; One key
    Due chiav**i**   -   Two key**s**.

Before you continue with the lessons in this book, we recommend that you write the examples above on a separate sheet of paper. Take a look at it whenever you have any doubt as to what plural ending you should use.

NOTE: The expression **C'è...** is always followed by a singular word or expression: *C'è una bambina dentro la casa.* But before a plural word or expression, the plural form **Ci sono...** (*There are*) must be used: *Ci sono due bambine dentro la casa.*

The expression **C'è** has a negative form: - **Non c'è**...

- **Non c'è** una sedia dentro la casa.

- **There is no** chair in the house.

- OR: **There isn't** a chair in the house.

The negative form of the expression **Ci sono...** is **Non ci sono...**

- **Non ci sono** sedie dentro la casa.

- **There are no** chairs in the house.

Putting things together

Using the numbers from one to ten, you can write sentences like the ones below:

- Ci sono **quattro** sedie e **una** tavola dentro la casa.

- Ci sono **tre** bambine e **due** bambini dentro la casa.

- Dentro la casa, c'è **una** tavola, **quattro** sedie e **otto** finestre. [1]

[1] *Even though this sentence describes several objects, it is the singular expression C'è... which is used for the whole sentence, since it is directly followed by a singular expression (una tavola).*

Things to do - Lezione 3

Use a separate sheet of paper to write
the following expressions in Italian.

1. There are nine cats in the house.

2. There are no tables in the house.

3. There are three chairs and a dog in the house.

4. There is one boy and one girl in the house.

5. There are ten windows in the house.

Answers on page 42

NOTES

Lezione 4 - Forme, colori e aggettivi

(*Shapes, Colors, and Adjectives*)

Vocabulary

arancione	=	orange	marrone	=	brown
beige	=	beige	nero	=	black
bianco	=	white	rosa	=	pink
blu	=	blue	rosso	=	red
giallo	=	yellow	verde	=	green
grigio	=	grey	viola	=	purple

il cerchio	=	the circle	Un aereo	=	An airplane
l'ellisse	=	the ellipse	Un albero	=	A tree
il quadrato	=	the square	Uno[1] stadio	=	A stadium
il rettangolo	=	the rectangle	Uno[1] zaino	=	A backpack
il triangolo	=	the triangle	[1] *See page 17.*		

Adjectives

Adjectives are used to describe words. In Italian, an adjective agrees in gender (*masculine or feminine*) and number (*singular or plural*) with the word it describes:

- Un quadrato ross**o**   -   A red square (*m.*)
- Una tavola ross**a**   -   A red table (*f.*)

When the masculine singular form of an adjective ends with **O**, its feminine form ends with **A**, as in the example above.

When the masculine singular form of an adjective ends with the letter **E**, there is no change in the feminine:

- Un quadrato **verde** e una tavola **verde**. [1]

[1] *Most adjectives in Italian come **after** the word they describe.*

NOTE: *The colors **beige, blu, rosa,** and **viola,** are invariable:*
- *Tre ellissi **blu** e due quadrati **viola**.*

NOTE: When saying the name of a color by itself, the masculine singular definite article **IL** is always used:

- **Il** marrone, **Il** verde, **Il** blu, etc...

Which means that the name of a color, when used to describe only the color itself, is always a masculine singular noun.

NOTE: When the definite articles **IL** and **LA** come before a noun beginning with a vowel, they are replaced with **L'**:

- **L'** arancione (*masculine*)
- **L'** ellisse (*feminine*)

- *See page 17 for complete tables of definite and indefinite articles.*

The Plural Forms of Adjectives

The formation of the plural adjectives in Italian follows the same rules as the nouns (*see page 12*):

- Un triangolo rosso e due triangoli rossi.

- Un quadrato grigio e due quadrati grigi. [1]

- Un cerchio bianco e due cerchi bianchi. [2]

- Un' ellisse bianca e due ellissi bianche. [3]

- Un triangolo verde e due triangoli verdi.

[1] Some singular words ending with the letters **IO** (as *grigio*), have only one **I** in the plural (*as grigi*).

But: - una tavol**a** grigi**a** e due tavol**e** grigi**e**.
(*the adjective **grigia** does not end with io, but with ia*)

[2] Some singular words ending with the letters **CO** (as *bianco*), end with the letters **CHI** in the plural (as *bianchi*).

[3] When a singular word ends with the letters **CA** (as *bianca*), the plural form of that word ends with the letters **CHE** (as *bianche*).

A. The Definite Article

The Italian definite article agrees in gender and number with the word it precedes, according to the examples below:

Il + m. sg. noun beginning with a consonant:	**Il** bambino.
Plural:	**I** bambini.
L' + m. sg. noun beginning with a vowel:	**L'**aereo.
Plural:	**Gli** aerei.
Lo + m. sg. noun beginning with Z:	**Lo** zaino.
Plural:	**Gli** zaini.
Lo + m. sg. noun beginning with S + consonant:	**Lo** stadio.
Plural:	**Gli** stadi.
La + **f**. sg. noun beginning with a consonant:	**La** bambina.
Plural:	**Le** bambine.
L' + **f**. sg. noun beginning with a vowel:	**L'**ellisse.
Plural:	**Le** ellissi.

B. The Indefinite Article

The Italian indefinite article agrees in gender and number with the word it precedes, according to the examples below:

Un + m. sg. noun beginning with a consonant:	**Un** bambino.
Plural:	**Dei** bambini.
Un + m. sg. noun beginning with a vowel:	**Un** albero.
Plural:	**Degli** alberi.
Uno + m. sg. noun beginning with Z:	**Uno** zaino.
Plural:	**Degli** zaini.
Uno + m. sg. noun beginning with S + consonant:	**Uno** stadio.
Plural:	**Degli** stadi.
Una + **f**. sg. noun beginning with a consonant:	**Una** bambina.
Plural:	**Delle** bambine.
Un' + **f**. sg. noun beginning with a vowel:	**Un'** ellisse.
Plural:	**Delle** ellissi.

About the Plural Indefinite Article

Although there is no exact English equivalent for the Italian plural indefinite article, it may nevertheless be translated as SOME, or A FEW, in many instances.

- **Dei** bambini e **delle** bambine.

  - *Some boys and a few girls.*
  - Or: *A few boys and some girls.*

- Ci sono **degli** zaini.

  - *There are some backpacks.*
  - Or: *There are a few backpacks.*

Things to do - Lezione 4

Use a separate sheet of paper to write
the following expressions in Italian.

1. There is one yellow triangle.

2. There are three purple ellipses.

3. There are eight red chairs in the house.

4. There is a blue rectangle and seven grey ellipses.

Answers on page 42

Lezione 5 - Soggetti e verbi - (*Subjects and Verbs*)

Vocabulary

è	=	is	La gatta =	The (*female*) cat
sono	=	are	non =	not
Lei	=	She		
Lui	=	He		
Loro	=	They (*m. & f.*)		
sopra	=	on; upon		
sotto	=	under; below		

Subjects and Verbs

• A verb can be preceded by either a noun or a pronoun:

Il bambino è dentro la casa.   (**bambino** is a **noun**)
 - The **boy** is in the house.

Lui è dentro la casa.   (**Lui** is a **pronoun**)
 - **He** is in the house.

A pronoun is a word which stands for a noun and refers to it
(as **Lui** refers to **bambino**, for example).

• Use the plural pronoun **Loro** to refer to plural nouns:

 - **Le bambine** sono dentro la casa. **Loro** sono dentro la casa.

• The subject pronouns **Lui, Lei**, and **Loro** are used only with people:

 - **I cani** sono sotto la tavola. Sono sotto la tavola.

However, **Loro** is used when referring to a group composed of
people and animals:

 - La bambina e il cane: - **Loro** sono dentro la casa.

19

The Negative

To write a negative sentence, simply write **NON** before the verb:

- **Non** siamo dentro la casa.   - *We are **not** in the house.*

Remember, however, that in the expressions **Non c'è...** and **Non ci sono...**, the **NON** comes before the whole expression, and not right before the verb:

- **Non c'è** un bambino dentro la casa.

- **Non ci sono** bambine dentro la casa.

Putting things together

Using what you have learned so far, you can now write longer sentences, and even small paragraphs:

C'è una gatta bianca e un cane marrone sopra la sedia. Il cane è sopra la sedia, e la gatta è sopra la sedia. Sono sopra la sedia.

Things to do - Lezione 5

Use a separate sheet of paper to write the following paragraph in Italian.

In the house there is a boy, a table, and a chair. The boy is on the chair, and the chair is not under the table. The boy, the table, and the chair are in the house. They are in the house.

Answers on page 43

Lezione 6 - Essere o non essere

(*To Be or Not To Be*)

Vocabulary
americano	=	American
italiano	=	Italian

The Italian equivalent of the verb TO BE is **ESSERE**:

subject pronouns	ESSERE			
io	sono		I	am
tu	sei		you	are
lui; lei	è		he; she	is
noi	siamo		we	are
voi [1]	siete		you	are
loro	sono [2]		they	are

[1] Both **Tu** and **Voi** are translated as YOU in English. In Italian, however, the subject pronoun **Tu** is used only when talking to one person, whereas the pronoun **Voi** is used to talk to **more** than one person.

[2] Notice how **SONO** is used with both io and loro.

Subject Pronouns in Italian

It is not necessary to use the subject pronouns in Italian, since each verb form usually differs from all the others. Use a subject pronoun to either clarify or emphasize the subject of the verb:

- Non sei dentro la casa, ma **io** sono dentro la casa.

- *You* are not in the house, but **I** am in the house.

NOTE: The pronouns NOI, VOI, and LORO can refer to groups that are composed of both masculine and feminine subjects:

- **Noi** siamo bambini e bambine.

- **Voi** siete bambini e bambine.

- **Loro** sono bambini e bambine.

Adjectives and Adjectives as Nouns

◆ The words **americano** and **italiano** are adjectives, and they therefore agree in gender and number with the words they describe:

- C'è una bambin**a** italian**a** dentro la casa. [1]

- Ci sono due bambin**i** american**i** dentro la casa.

[1] *Italian adjectives are not capitalized.*

◆ Italian adjectives can also be used as nouns:

- Gli italian**i** sono dentro la casa.   - *The Italians are in the house.*

Things to do - Lezione 6

Write your answers to the exercises below on a separate sheet of paper

   A. Write the sentences below in the right order.

    1. bambina / La / americana. / è
    2. e / sono / bambino / americani. / bambina / Il / la
    3. non / italiani. / sono / Loro
    4. non / sotto / quadrato / è / l'ellisse. / Il
    5. il / dentro / triangolo. / È

   B. Complete the sentences below with the proper forms of the the given adjectives. Watch out for gender and number !

   1. Siamo _____. (americano, *m.*)

     Non siamo _____. (italiano, *m.*)

   2. La bambina è _____. (italiano)

     Lei non è _____. (americano)

   3. L'aereo è _____ e la tavola è _____. (blu, blu)

   4. L'ellisse e il triangolo sono _____. (verde)

     Non sono _____. (viola)

   C. Write the following sentences in **Italian**.

   1. The three girls are American. They are not Italian.

   2. The five white ellipses are in the house. They are not on the table.

   3. The rectangle is not in the triangle. It is under the circle.

   4. The yellow tables are not in the house.

Answers on pages 43-44

Elementary Italian Grammar for Reading and Writing

Lezione 7 - Saluti — (*Greetings*)

Vocabulary

Ciao	=	Hello
Buongiorno	=	Good day; Hello
Arrivederci	=	Good bye
Signora	=	Ma'am; Mrs.
Signore [1]	=	Mister; Sir
Mi chiamo...	=	My name is... (lit. *I call myself...*)
Come va ?	=	How are you doing ?
E tu ?	=	And you ?
E Lei ?	=	And you ? (*polite form*), (m. & f.)
Va bene	=	I am doing well; It's going well
Grazie	=	Thank you
A presto	=	Until then; See you soon

[1] When SIGNORE comes right before a man's last name, it is
written without the E at the end: - Buongiorno, **Signor** Verdi !

A Greeting Parenthesis

It may be somewhat awkward to start speaking to someone you
don't know without having made the proper introductions.   In
Italian culture, talking to someone without having first exchanged
some form of greetings is often considered inappropriate.   The
two forms of greetings shown below and on the next page are
appropriate in most any situation. Such greetings are an ideal way
to *break the ice* in Italian.

I. Informal greetings: Paolo and Caterina

Paolo	- Ciao ! Mi chiamo Paolo.
Caterina	- Buongiorno, Paolo ! Mi chiamo Caterina.
Paolo	- Come va, Caterina ?
Caterina	- Va bene, grazie. E tu ?
Paolo	- Va bene, grazie.
Caterina	- Arrivederci, Paolo !
Paolo	- Arrivederci, Caterina. A presto !

II. Formal greetings: Mr. Luigi Nardi and Mrs. Laura Campi

Mr. Nardi
- Buongiorno, Signora. Mi chiamo Luigi Nardi.

Mrs. Campi
- Buongiorno, Signor Nardi. Mi chiamo Laura Campi.

Mr. Nardi
- Come va, Signora Campi ?

Mrs. Campi
- Va bene, grazie. E Lei ?

Mr. Nardi
- Va bene, grazie.

Mrs. Campi
- A presto, Signor Nardi !

Mr. Nardi
- A presto, Signora Campi !

Things to do - Lezione 7

Write your answers on a separate sheet of paper

A. Write the following sentences in Italian.

1. My name is Caterina.
2. Hello, Paolo. How are you ?
3. I am doing well, Mr. Nardi, thank you.
4. See you soon, Mrs. Campi.

B. Write the following sentences in **English**.

1. Come va, Caterina ?
2. Va bene, grazie.
3. Buongiorno, Signora Campi.
4. A presto, Paolo !

Answers on page 45

Lezione 8 - Che cosa è ?

(What is that ?)

Vocabulary

che	=	what
cosa	=	thing
dove	=	where
no	=	no
non	=	not
si	=	yes
questo	=	this; that
il camino	=	the chimney
la cucitrice	=	the stapler
la forchetta	=	the fork
la matita	=	the pencil
la penna	=	the pen
il piatto	=	the plate
la scrivania	=	the desk
il tetto	=	the roof

The interrogative

When learning a new language, the ability to ask simple questions is an efficient and powerful tool to acquire new vocabulary and further your mastery of that language.

◆ To find out the name of a specific object, the most common question to ask is **Che cosa è ?**

- **Che cosa è ?**   - What is this ? / What is *that* ?

- È una scrivania.   - It's a desk.

◆ To further inquire about an object, you may use **È... ?**

- **È** una tavola ?   - *Is (that; or: it) a table ?*

- No. Non è una tavola. È una scrivania.

- No, It's not a table. It's a desk.

◆ The same question can be asked with **SONO** to inquire about more than one object:

- **Sono matite ?**

- Are (*these things; or: they*) pencils ?

- Si, sono matite.

- Yes, (*these things; or: they*) are pencils.

◆ While pointing to an object, you may ask the following question:

- **E questo, che cosa è ?**   - And that, what is it ?

- **È** una cucitrice.   - It's a stapler.

◆ You can combine **Dove** with a form of the verb **ESSERE** to inquire about the location of an object (*or a person*):

- **Dov'** è la penna ?   - **Where** is the pen ?
(*dove + è = dov' è*)

◆ You can also begin a question with a form of the verb **ESSERE** to find out if an object is in a specific place:

- **È** il piatto sopra la tavola ?   - **Is** the plate on the table ?

◆ Finally, you can use the interrogative expression **Che cosa c'è** to ask what object there is in a certain place:

- **Che cosa c'è** sopra la tavola ?   - What is (*there*) on the table ?

- **C'è** un piatto sopra la tavola.   - There is a plate on the table.

Things to do - Lezione 8

Write your answers to the exercises below on a separate sheet of paper.
Refer to the examples above to help you complete this section.

A. Write the answers to the following questions.
Use the information given between parentheses.

1. Dove sono le forchette ? (*sopra la tavola*)
2. È il gatto sopra la tavola ? (*no, sotto la tavola*)
3. Che cosa c'è dentro la casa ? (*una tavola e quattro sedie*)
4. Sono gatti ? (*no, gatte*)

B. Write the questions that would elicit the answers below.

1. È un quadrato.
2. No. Non è un gatto. È un cane.
3. Si, il bambino è dentro la casa.
4. C'è un camino sopra il tetto.
5. Le bambine americane ? Sono dentro la casa.

Answers on page 46

NOTES

Elementary Italian Grammar for Reading and Writing

Lezione 9 - Un po' di aritmetica (*Some Arithmetic*)

Vocabulary

undici	=	eleven	sedici	=	sixteen
dodici	=	twelve	diciassette	=	seventeen
tredici	=	thirteen	diciotto	=	eighteen
quattordici	=	fourteen	diciannove	=	nineteen
quindici	=	fifteen	venti	=	twenty

più	=	plus (+)	diviso	=	divided *by* (÷)
meno	=	minus (-)	una chiave	=	a key
per	=	times (x)	un libro	=	a book
uguale	=	equals (=)			

Working with numbers

Working out even simple arithmetic operations in a new language may at first appear quite daunting. But this perceived difficulty can quickly disappear by following the few simple rules given below.

1. **Addizione** - *Addition*

To add two numbers together, simply use the words **più** and **uguale**:

- Uno **più** uno **uguale** due.   - One **plus** one **equals** two.

2. **Sottrazione** - *Substraction*

To substract one number from another, use **meno** and **uguale**:

- Tre **meno** due **uguale** uno.   - Three **minus** two **equals** one.

3. **Moltiplicazione** - *Multiplication*

To multiply a number by another, use the words **per** and **uguale**:

- Quattro **per** cinque **uguale** venti.   - Four **times** five **equals** twenty.

4. **Divisione** - *Division*

To divide a number by another, use **diviso** and **uguale**:

- Dieci **diviso** due **uguale** cinque.   - Ten **divided** *by* two **equals** five.

Things to do - Lezione 9

Write your answers to the exercises below on a separate sheet of paper.

A. Write the operations below with **words.**

(5 + 6 = 11)

(9 - 4 = 5)

(3 x 4 = 12)

(18 ÷ 9 = 2)

B. Write the operations below with **numbers.**

(Diciotto più due uguale venti)

(Diciannove meno dodici uguale sette)

(Otto per due uguale sedici)

(Venti diviso cinque uguale quattro)

C. Write the following sentences in **Italian.**

1. Fifteen blue books minus three blue books equals twelve blue books.

2. Nine grey keys plus five grey keys equals fourteen grey keys.

3. Ten times two equals twenty.

4. Eighteen divided by three equals six.

Answers on page 47

Lezione 10
I giorni della settimana e il verbo ANDARE
(The Days of the Week and the Verb TO GO)

Vocabulary

la banca	=	the bank	dopo	=	after
la biblioteca	=	the library	ma	=	but
la chiesa	=	the church	il giorno	=	the day
la farmacia	=	the drugstore	la mattina	=	the morning
Roma	=	Rome	il pomeriggio	=	the afternoon
la scuola	=	the school	la sera	=	the evening
il teatro	=	the theater	la notte	=	the night
anche	=	also	la settimana	=	the week
della	=	of the (*+ f.*)	il primo	=	the first

Il verbo ANDARE

vado	=	I go	andiamo	=	we go
vai	=	you go	andate	=	you go [1]
va	=	he goes; she goes	vanno	=	they go

[1] Remember to use **VAI** when talking to one person, and **ANDATE** when talking to more than one person.

- -

The verb **ANDARE** can also be translated as **TO BE GOING**

vado	=	I am going
vai	=	you are going
etc...		

- -

When the verb **ANDARE** is used to indicate that the subject is going from one place to another, it is followed by one of two prepositions, **a** or **in**:

- Vado **a** scuola.   - I am going **to** (*a*) school.

- Andiamo **in** banca   - We are going **to** (*a*) bank.

The Prepositions A and IN

The prepositions A and IN have a similar meaning when used after the verb ANDARE. *Andare a...* and *Andare in...*, when followed by a place (destination), both mean *Going to / Going towards...*.

Although the preposition **A** is more often used before a location that is seen as a specific place (*e.g. a city*), and **IN** before a location that is seen as a general area (*e.g. a country*), the choice of preposition in the expressions below has been set more by usage than by a strict application of the rule stated above. In that respect, they have more in common with idiomatic expressions [1] than with a strict application of grammatical rules.

In this lesson, the following expressions are used:

Andare a casa	=	Going home, to one's house
Andare a scuola	=	Going to school
Andare a teatro	=	Going to the theater
Andare a Roma	=	Going to Rome
Andare in banca	=	Going to (*a*) bank
Andare in biblioteca	=	Going to (*a*) library
Andare in chiesa	=	Going to (*a*) church
Andare in farmacia	=	Going to (*a*) drugstore

[1] *An idiomatic expression is an expression whose meaning as a whole often does not depend on the meaning of the individual words that make up that expression (For example, the meaning of the expression "What's up?" in English –as a greeting- cannot be guessed from its individual parts). Consequently, each idiomatic expression in Italian must be learned as a whole.*

NOTE: More details on prepositions will be given as they are used in subsequent lessons (*levels II and III*).

The Days of the Week

In Italian, the days of the week are named as follows:

- lunedì, martedì, mercoledì, giovedì, venerdì, sabato, domenica.

- Monday, Tuesday, Wednesday, Thursday, Friday, Saturday, Sunday.

The days of the week are not capitalized in Italian, except when they are part of a holiday's name:

- **V**enerdi Santo. - Good Friday.

Naturally, when a day of the week begins a sentence, it is always capitalized:

- Lunedì e martedì sono i due primi giorni della settimana.
- *Monday and Tuesday are the first two days of the week.*

The days of the week in Italian are all masculine nouns, save for **Domenica**, which is a feminine noun.

When talking about something that happens more or less regularly on a given day, the definite article IL (*or LA, for Domenica only*) comes before the day:

- La domenica, andiamo in chiesa.
  - Every Sunday, we go to church.
  - OR: We go to church on Sundays.

- Il lunedì, vado a scuola.
  - Every Monday, I go to school.
  - OR: I go to school on Mondays.

First or Last ? Depending on what tradition one follows, either Sunday or Monday is considered the first day of the week. For centuries, due to the long standing Catholic tradition in Italy, Sunday was considered the first day of the week. More often nowadays, it is Monday which is counted as the first day, since it begins the work week.

Putting things together

Using the verb ANDARE and the days of the week, along with the vocabulary for this lesson, you can read and write sentences like the ones below:

Ci sono sette giorni **in** una settimana.

(*The Italian* **in** *means the same as the English* **in**)

Lunedì, martedì, mercoledì, giovedì, venerdì, sabato
e domenica sono i sette giorni della settimana.

In un giorno, c'è la mattina, il pomeriggio e la sera.

Dopo la sera, c'è la notte.

Io vado a scuola il lunedì mattina. [1]

Anche tu vai a scuola ?   - (*Are you* **also** *going to school ?*)

Tu vai in farmacia il martedì pomeriggio,

... ma io vado in farmacia il mercoledì mattina.

Lei va a Roma sabato.

Andiamo in banca mercoledì.

Non andate in biblioteca il venerdì ?

Vanno a teatro il sabato sera.

Paolo e Caterina vanno in chiesa la domenica mattina.

[1] Use the words **mattina, pomeriggio, sera**, or **notte** right after a day of the week to indicate which part of the day you are talking about : (*Mercoledì sera = Wednesday evening*).

Things to do - Lezione 10

Write your answers to the exercises below
on a separate sheet of paper.

A. Write the sentences below in the right order.

1. in banca / il mercoledì. / Andiamo
2. a scuola / mattina. / Tu vai / il lunedì
3. vanno / Loro / Roma / venerdì. / a
4. giovedì / Andate / il / in / pomeriggio. / farmacia

B. Complete the following sentences with the words given below.

1. Paolo e Caterina _____ a scuola il lunedì _____.

2. Loro vanno ___ casa il _____ pomeriggio.

3. Il sabato, Paolo va a _____ , ___ Caterina _____ in biblioteca.

4. Io ___ vado a scuola ____ lunedì sera.

5. E _____ , _____ vai a _____ ?

a, lunedì, vanno, teatro, e, il, anche, mattina, va, non, tu, scuola

C. Write the following sentences in **English.**

1. Caterina va in banca il martedì mattina.
2. Paolo e Caterina non vanno a teatro il venerdì pomeriggio.
3. Io vado a casa, ma tu vai in biblioteca.
4. Ci sono sette giorni in una settimana.

D. Write the following sentences in **Italian.**

1. Do you go to school every Wednesday ? (use **vai**)
2. We are not going to the library Tuesday afternoon.
3. They are going to the bank Friday morning.
4. The girl goes home every Saturday.

Answers on pages 48-49

Elementary Italian Grammar for Reading and Writing

Risposte

Answers

Elementary Italian Grammar for Reading and Writing

Answers to Things to do - Lezione 1

1.	The dog	—	Il cane
2.	The girl	—	La bambina
3.	The cat	—	Il gatto
4.	The boy	—	Il bambino
5.	The cat and the dog	—	Il gatto e il cane
6.	The girl and the boy	—	La bambina e il bambino
7.	The dog and the cat	—	Il cane e il gatto
8.	The boy and the girl	—	Il bambino e la bambina

Answers to Things to do - Lezione 2

1. There is a cat in the house.
   — C'è un gatto dentro la casa.

2. There is a girl and a dog in the house.
   — C'è una bambina e un cane dentro la casa.

3. There is a boy in the house.
   — C'è un bambino dentro la casa.

4. There is one cat and one dog in the house.
   — C'è un gatto e un cane dentro la casa.

Answers to Things to do - Lezione 3

1. There are nine cats in the house.
   — Ci sono nove gatti dentro la casa.

2. There are no tables in the house.
   — Non ci sono tavole dentro la casa.

3. There are three chairs and a dog in the house.
   — Ci sono tre sedie e un cane dentro la casa.

4. There is one boy and one girl in the house.
   — C'è un bambino e una bambina dentro la casa.

5. There are ten windows in the house.
   — Ci sono dieci finestre dentro la casa.

Answers to Things to do - Lezione 4

1. There is one yellow triangle.
   — C'è un triangolo giallo.

2. There are three purple ellipses.
   — Ci sono tre ellissi viola.
   (*see the note at the bottom of page 15*)

3. There are eight red chairs in the house.
   — Ci sono otto sedie rosse dentro la casa.

4. There is a blue rectangle and seven grey ellipses.
   — C'è un rettangolo blu e sette ellissi grigie.

Answers to Things to do - Lezione 5

In the house there is a boy, a table, and a chair. The boy is on the chair, and the chair is not under the table. The boy, the table, and the chair are in the house. They are in the house.

Dentro la casa c'è un bambino, una tavola e una sedia. Il bambino è sopra la sedia, e la sedia non è sotto la tavola. Il bambino, la tavola e la sedia sono dentro la casa. Sono dentro la casa. (or: **Loro** *sono*...).

Answers to Things to do - Lezione 6

A. Write the sentences below in the right order.

1. bambina / La / americana. / è
   - La bambina è americana.

2. e / sono / bambino / americani. / bambina / Il / la
   - Il bambino e la bambina sono americani.

3. non / italiani. / sono / Loro
   - Loro non sono italiani.

4. non / sotto / quadrato / è / l'ellisse. / Il
   - Il quadrato non è sotto l'ellisse.

5. il / dentro / triangolo. / È
   - È dentro il triangolo.

B. Complete each sentence with the proper form of the given adjectives. Watch out for gender and number !

1. Siamo **americani**.

   Non siamo **italiani**.

2. La bambina è **italiana**.

   Lei non è **americana**.

3. L'aereo è **blu** e la tavola è **blu**. - (*see note on page 15*)

4. L'ellisse e il triangolo sono **verdi**.

   Non sono **viola**. - (*see note on page 15*)

C. Write the following sentences in Italian.

1. The three girls are American. They are not Italian.
   - Le tre bambin**e** sono american**e**. Non sono italian**e**.

2. The five white ellipses are in the house. They are not on the table.
   - Le cinque elliss**i** bian**che** sono dentro la casa.
     Non sono sopra la tavola.

3. The rectangle is not in the triangle. It is under the circle.
   - Il rettangolo non è dentro il triangolo. È sotto il cerchio.

4. The yellow tables are not in the house.
   - Le tavol**e** gial**le** non sono dentro la casa.

Answers to Things to do - Lezione 7

A. Write the following sentences in Italian.

1. My name is Caterina.
   - Mi chiamo Caterina.

2. Hello, Paolo. How are you ?
   - Ciao, Paolo. Come va ?

3. I am doing well, Mr. Nardi, thank you.
   - Va bene, Signor Nardi, grazie.

4. See you soon, Mrs. Campi.
   - A presto, Signora Campi.

B. Write the following sentences in **English**.

1. Come va, Caterina ?
   - How are you, Caterina ?

2. Va bene, grazie.
   - I am doing well, thank you.

3. Buongiorno, Signora Campi.
   - Good day, Mrs. Campi.

4. A presto, Paolo !
   - See you soon, Paolo !

   - **Or**: Until then, Paolo !

Answers to Things to do - Lezione 8

A. Write the answers to the following questions.
Use the information given between parentheses.

1. Dove sono le forchette ? (*sopra la tavola*)
   - Le forchette sono sopra la tavola.
   - **Or**: Sono sopra la tavola.

2. È il gatto sopra la tavola ? (*no, sotto la tavola*)
   - No. Non è sopra la tavola. È sotto la tavola.
   - **Or**: No. È sotto la tavola.

3. Che cosa c'è dentro la casa ? (*una tavola e quattro sedie*)
   - C'è una tavola e quattro sedie dentro la casa.

4. Sono questi gatti ? (*no, gatt<u>e</u>*)
   - No, non sono gatti. Sono gatte.

B. Write the questions that would elicit the answers below.

1. È un quadrato.
   - Che cosa è ?

2. No. Non è un gatto. È un cane.
   - È un gatto ?

3. Si, il bambino è dentro la casa.
   - È il bambino dentro la casa ?

4. C'è un camino sopra il tetto.
   - Che cosa c'è sopra il tetto ?

5. Le bambine americane ? Sono dentro la casa.
   - Dove sono le bambine (*americane*) ?

Answers to Things to do - Lezione 9

A. Write the operations below with **words**

(5 + 6 = 11)   - Cinque più sei uguale undici.

(9 - 4 = 5)   - Nove meno quattro uguale cinque.

(3 x 4 = 12)   - Tre per quattro uguale dodici.

(18 ÷ 9 = 2)   - Diciotto diviso nove uguale due.

B. Write the operations below with **numbers**

(Diciotto più due uguale venti)   ◆   18 + 2 = 20

(Diciannove meno dodici uguale sette)   ◆   19 - 12 = 7

(Otto per due uguale sedici)   ◆   8 x 2 = 16

(Venti diviso cinque uguale quattro)   ◆   20 ÷ 5 = 4

C. Write the following sentences in **Italian**

1. Fifteen blue books minus three blue books equals twelve blue books.
   - Quindici libri blu meno tre libri blu uguale dodici libri blu.

2. Nine grey keys plus five grey keys equals fourteen grey keys.
   - Nove chiavi grigie più cinque chiavi grigie uguale quattordici chiavi grigie.

3. Ten times two equals twenty.
   - Dieci per due uguale venti.

4. Eighteen divided by three equals six.
   - Diciotto diviso tre uguale sei.

Answers to Things to do - Lezione 10

A. Write the sentences below in the right order.

1. in banca / il mercoledì. / Andiamo
   - Andiamo in banca il mercoledì.

2. a scuola / mattina. / Tu vai / il lunedì
   - Tu vai a scuola il lunedì mattina.

3. vanno / Loro / Roma / venerdì. / a
   - Loro vanno a Roma venerdì.

4. giovedì / Andate / il / in / pomeriggio. / farmacia
   - Andate in farmacia il giovedì pomeriggio.

B. Complete the following sentences with the words given below.

1. Paolo e Caterina **vanno** a scuola il lunedì **mattina**.

2. Loro vanno **a** casa il **lunedì** pomeriggio.

3. Il sabato, Paolo va a **teatro**, **e** Caterina **va** in biblioteca.

4. Io **non** vado a scuola **il** lunedì sera.

5. E **tu**, **anche** vai a **scuola** ?

a, lunedì, vanno, teatro, e, il, anche, mattina, va, non, tu, scuola

Answers to Things to do - Lezione 10 (*continued*)

C. Write the following sentences in **English.**

1. Caterina va in banca il martedì mattina.
   - Caterina goes to the bank every Tuesday morning.

2. Paolo e Caterina non vanno a teatro
   il venerdì pomeriggio.
   - Paolo and Caterina do not go to the theater
     on Friday afternoons.

3. Io vado a casa, ma tu vai in biblioteca.
   - I am going home, but you are going to the library.

4. Ci sono sette giorni in una settimana.
   - There are seven days in a week.
   - **Or**: There are seven days in *one* week.

D. Write the following sentences in **Italian.**

1. Do you go to school every Wednesday ? (use **vai**)
   - Vai a scuola il mercoledì ?

2. We are not going to the library Tuesday afternoon.
   - Non andiamo in biblioteca martedì pomeriggio.

3. They are going to the bank Friday morning.
   - Vanno in banca venerdì mattina.

4. The girl goes home every Saturday.
   - La bambina va a casa il sabato.

VOCABULARY

NOUNS

l'aereo	=	the airplane	la matita	=	the pencil
l'albero	=	the tree	la mattina	=	the morning
americano	=	American	la notte	=	the night
la bambina	=	the girl	la penna	=	the pen
il bambino	=	the boy	il piatto	=	the plate
la banca	=	the bank	il pomeriggio	=	the afternoon
la biblioteca	=	the library	il primo	=	the first
il camino	=	the chimney	il quadrato	=	the square
il cane	=	the dog	il rettangolo	=	the rectangle
la casa	=	the house	Roma	=	Rome
il cerchio	=	the circle	la scrivania	=	the desk
la chiave	=	the key	la scuola	=	the school
la chiesa	=	the church	la sedia	=	the chair
la cucitrice	=	the stapler	la sera	=	the evening
l'ellisse	=	the ellipse	la settimana	=	the week
la farmacia	=	the pharmacy	Signora	=	Ma'am; Mrs.
la finestra	=	the window	Signore	=	Sir; Mister
la forchetta	=	the fork	il stadio	=	the stadium
la gatta	=	the (*female*) cat	la tavola	=	the table
il gatto	=	the (*male*) cat	il teatro	=	the theatre
il giorno	=	the day	il tetto	=	the roof
italiano	=	Italian	il triangolo	=	the triangle
il libro	=	the book	il zaino	=	the backpack

NUMBERS FROM ONE TO TWENTY

uno, due, tre, quattro, cinque, sei, sette, otto, nove, dieci;

undici, dodici, tredici, quattordici, quindici,

sedici, diciassette, diciotto, diciannove, venti.

THE COLORS

arancione	=	orange	marrone	=	brown
beige	=	beige	nero	=	black
bianco	=	white	rosa	=	pink
blu	=	blue	rosso	=	red
giallo	=	yellow	verde	=	green
grigio	=	grey	viola	=	purple

VOCABULARY

MISCELLANEOUS WORDS AND EXPRESSIONS

a	=	to; at	questo	=	this; that
in	=	in			
			no	=	no
anche	=	also	non	=	not
			si	=	yes
della	=	of the (+ *fem.*)			
			che	=	what
e	=	and	cosa	=	thing
ma	=	but			
			dove	=	where
c'è...	=	there is...			
ci sono...	=	there are...	A presto	=	See you soon
			arrivederci	=	Good bye
dentro	=	in; within; inside	bene	=	well
sopra	=	on; upon	buongiorno	=	Good day
sotto	=	under; below	ciao	=	Hello
			Come	=	how
dopo	=	after	grazie	=	thank you
			Mi chiamo...	=	My name is...
diviso	=	divided by			
meno	=	minus			
per	=	by; times			
più	=	plus			
uguale	=	equals			

ARTICLES

il	=	the - (*m.*)		un	=	a - (*m.*)
la	=	the - (*f.*)		una	=	a - (*f.*)

SUBJECT PRONOUNS

io, tu, lei, lui, Lei, noi, voi, loro
I, you, she, he, You (formal), we, you (*pl.*), they

ANDARE: vado, vai, va, andiamo, andate, vanno
            I go, you go, he/she goes, we go, you go (*pl.*), they go

ESSERE: sono, sei, è, siamo, siete, sono
            I am, you are, he/she is, we are, you are (*pl.*), they are

INDEX

Made in the USA
Lexington, KY
05 June 2013